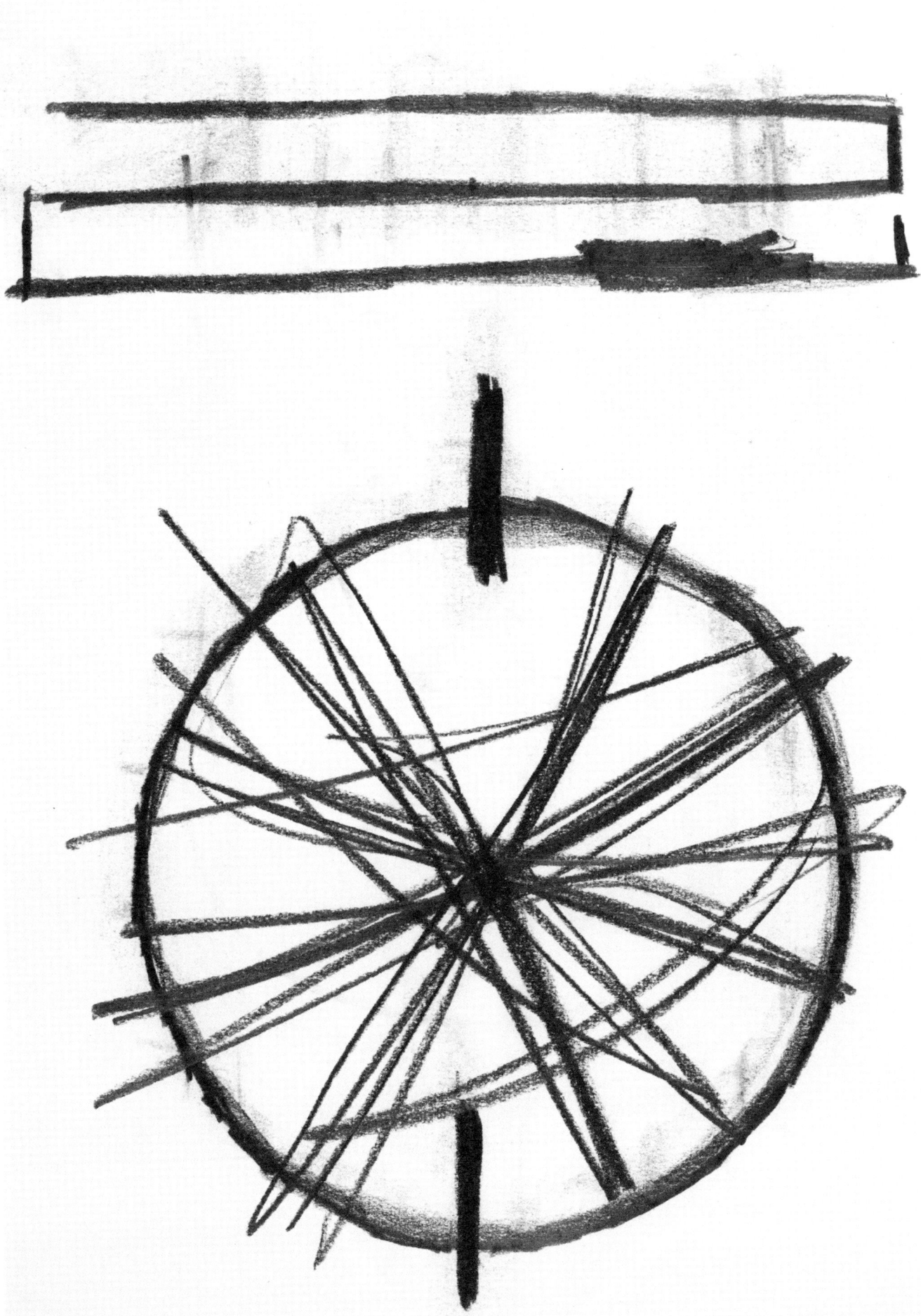

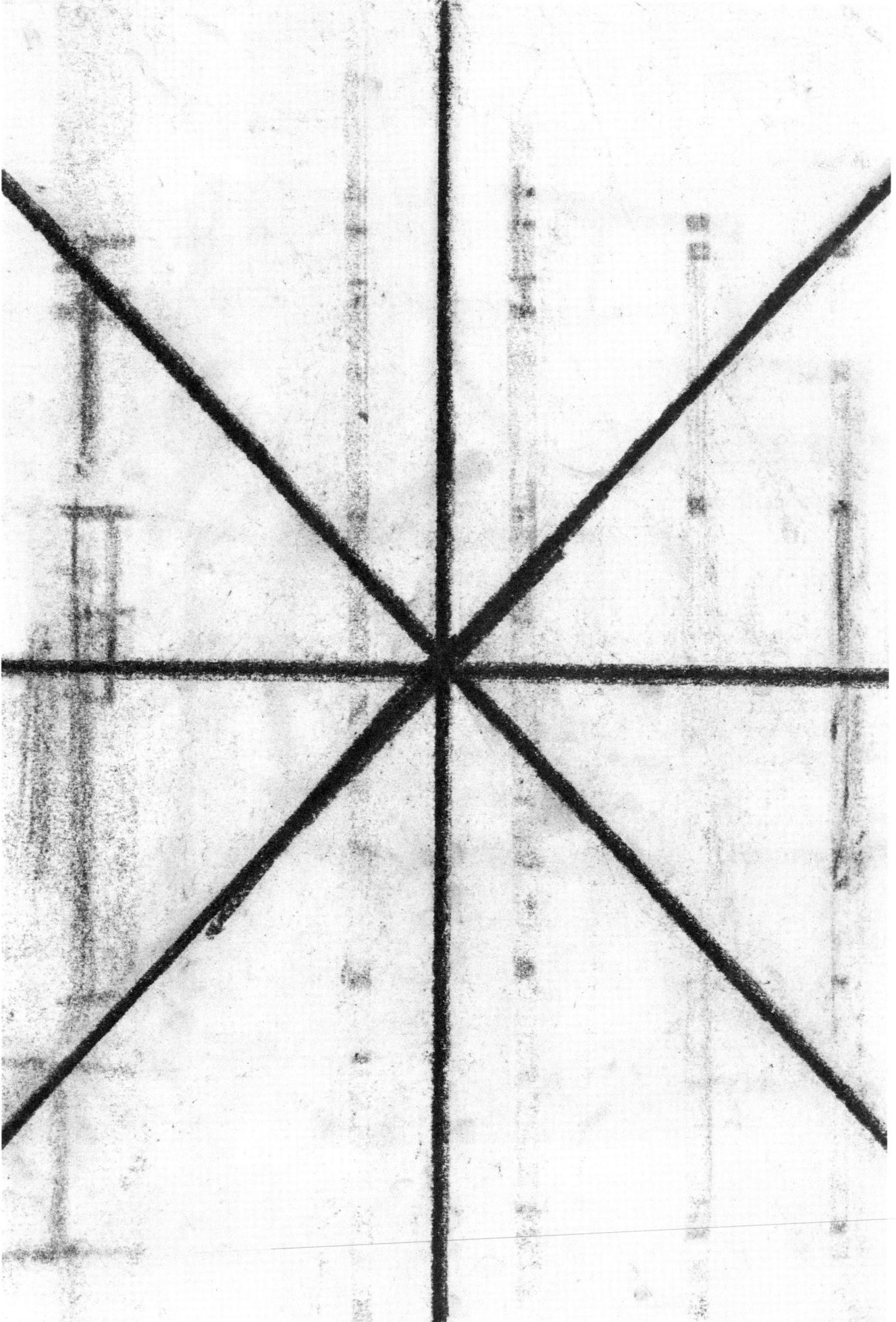

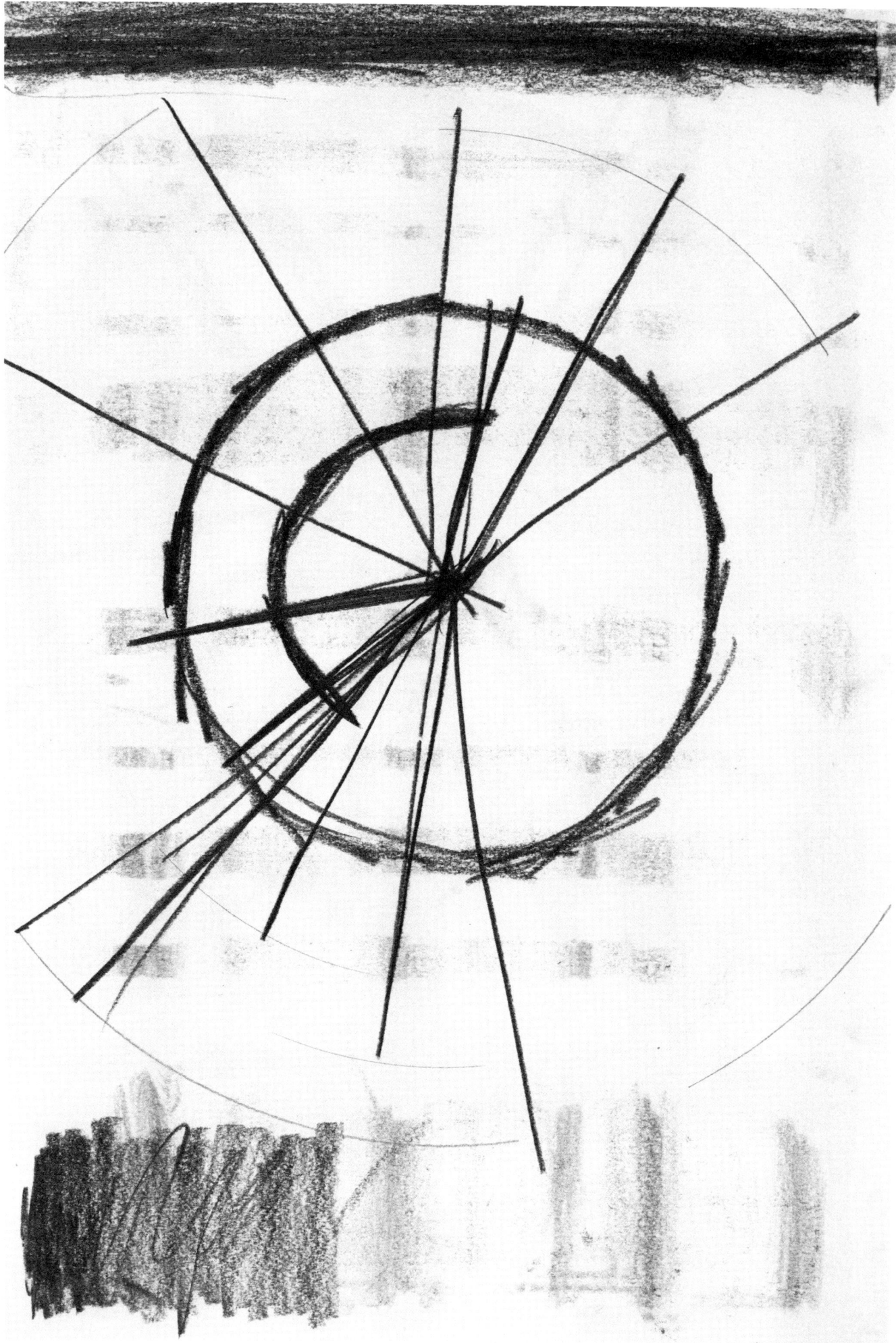

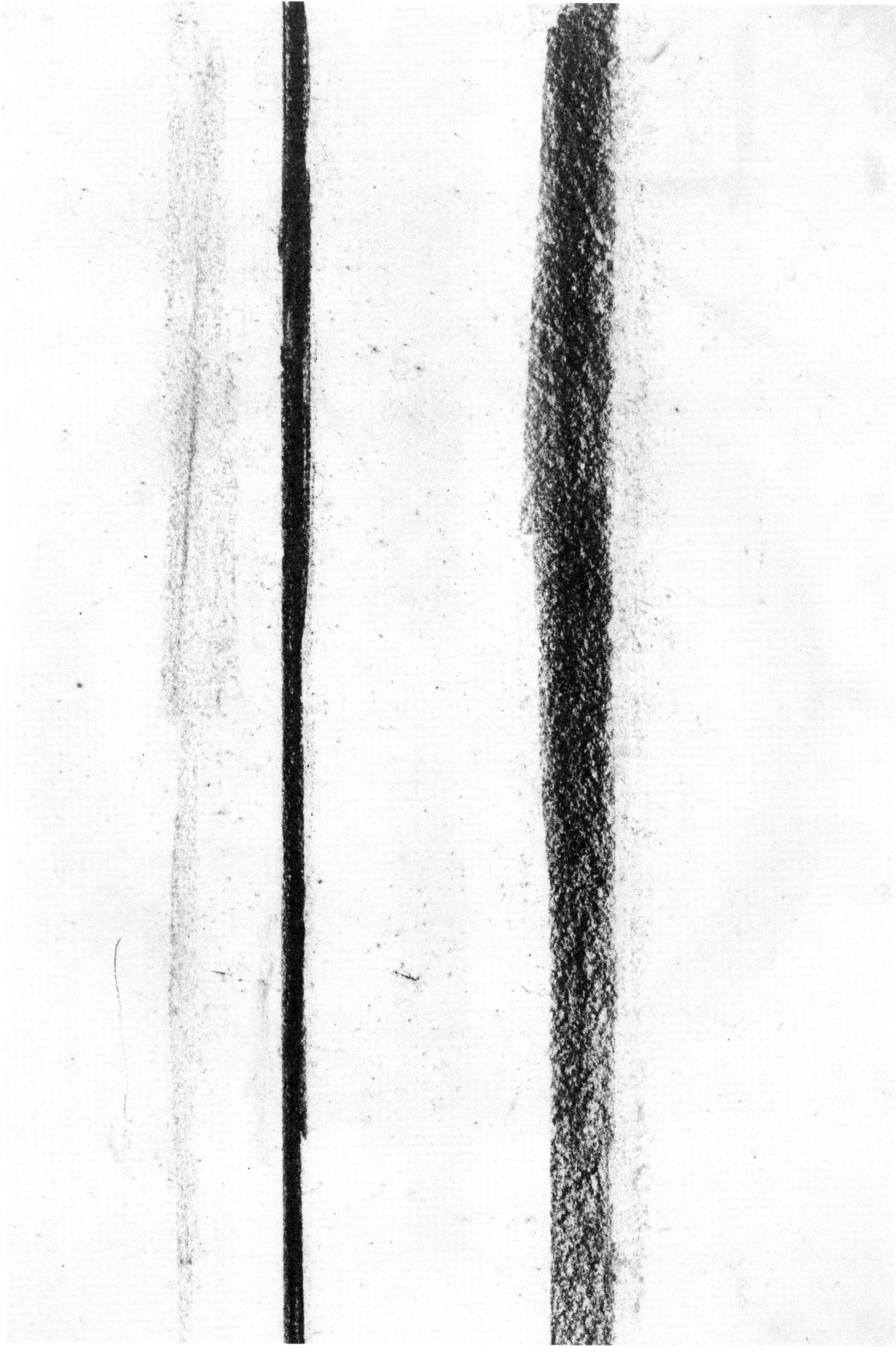

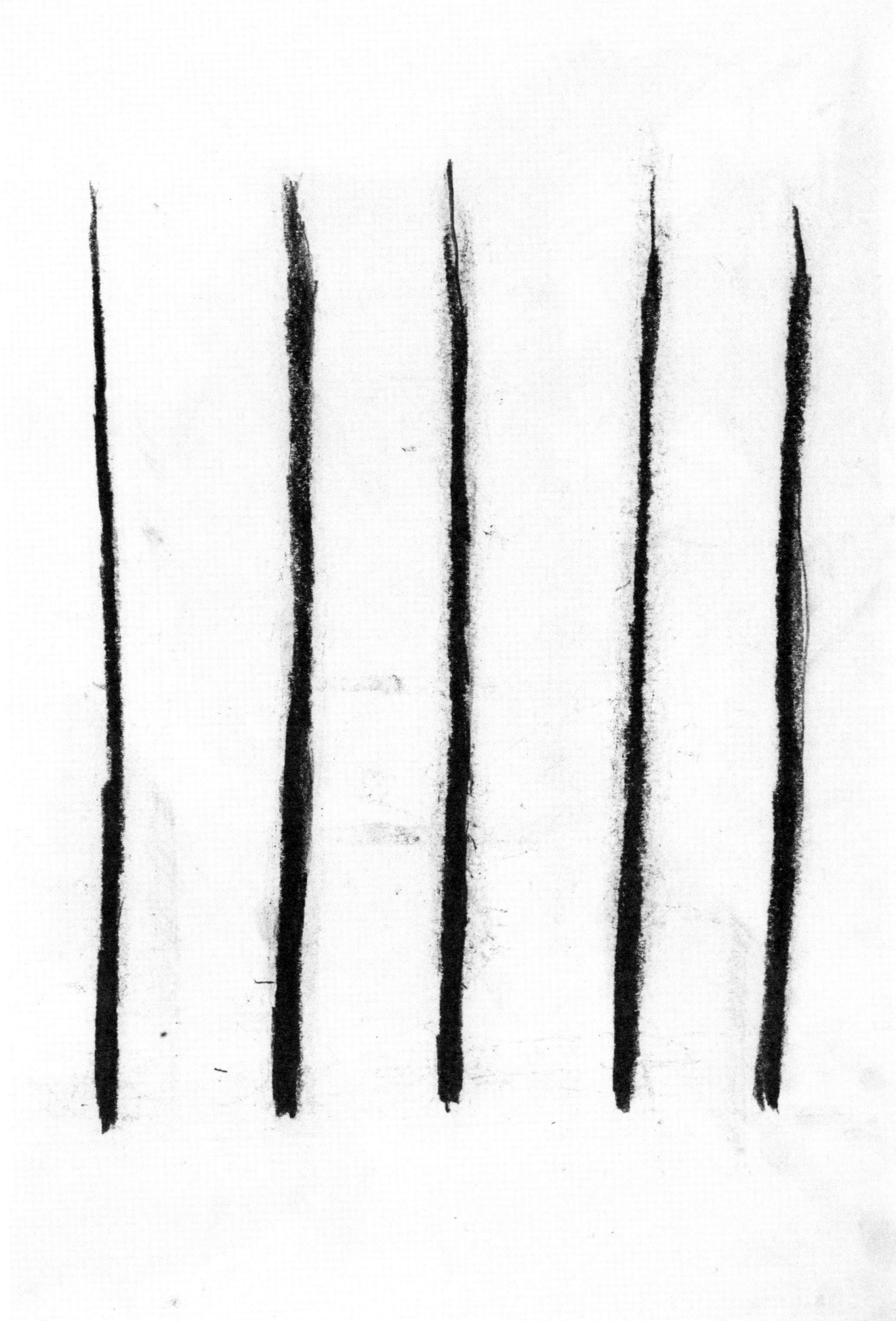

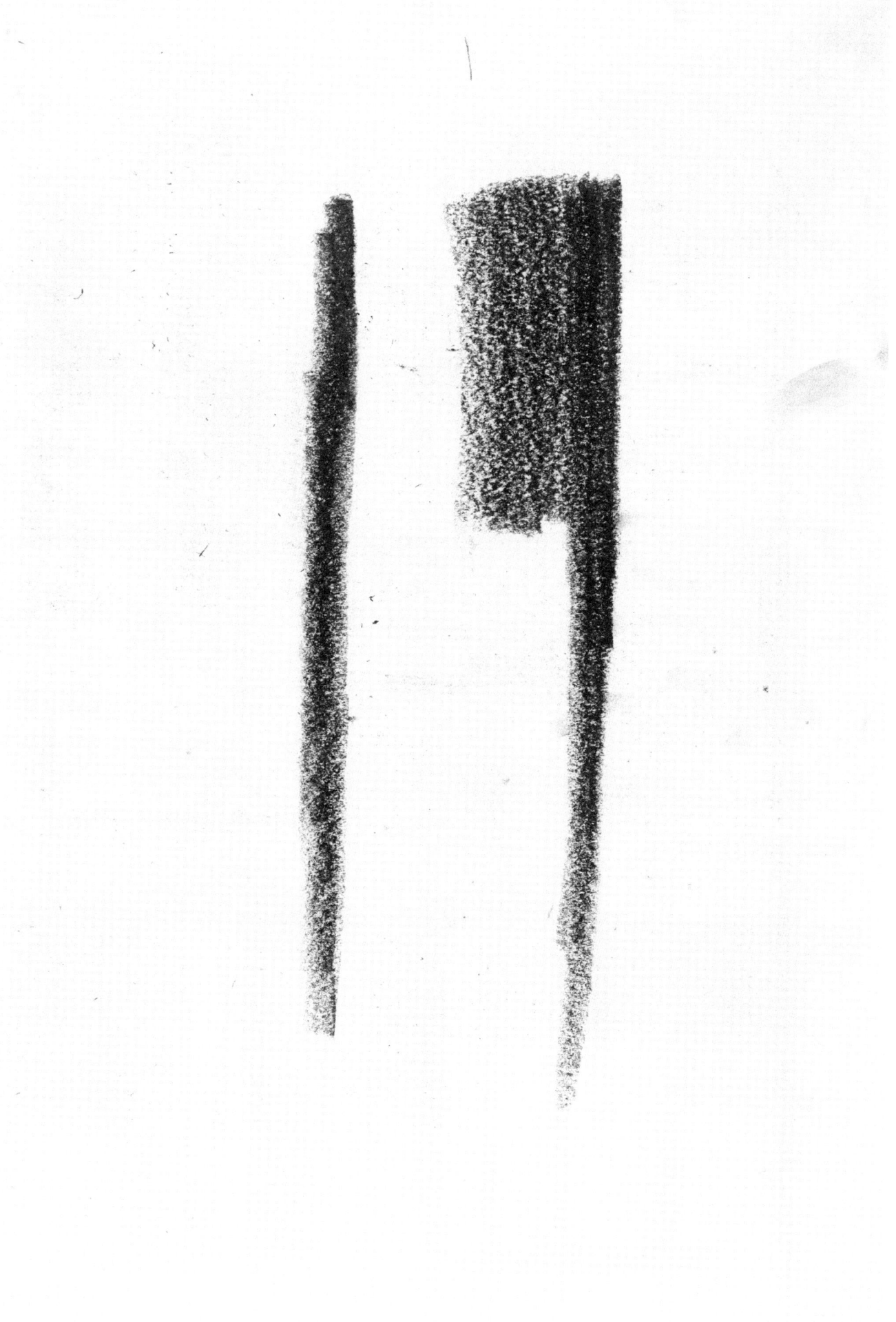

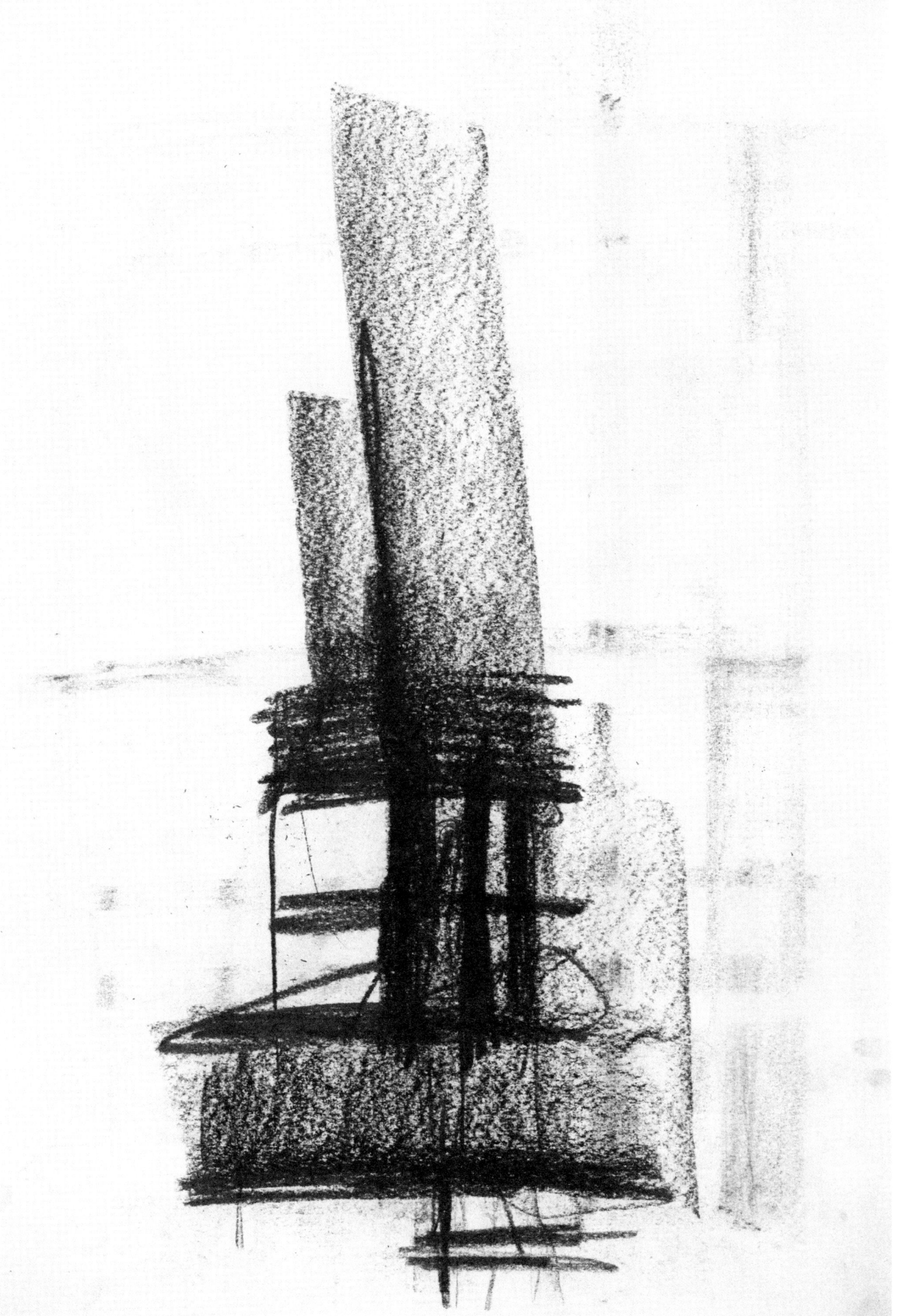

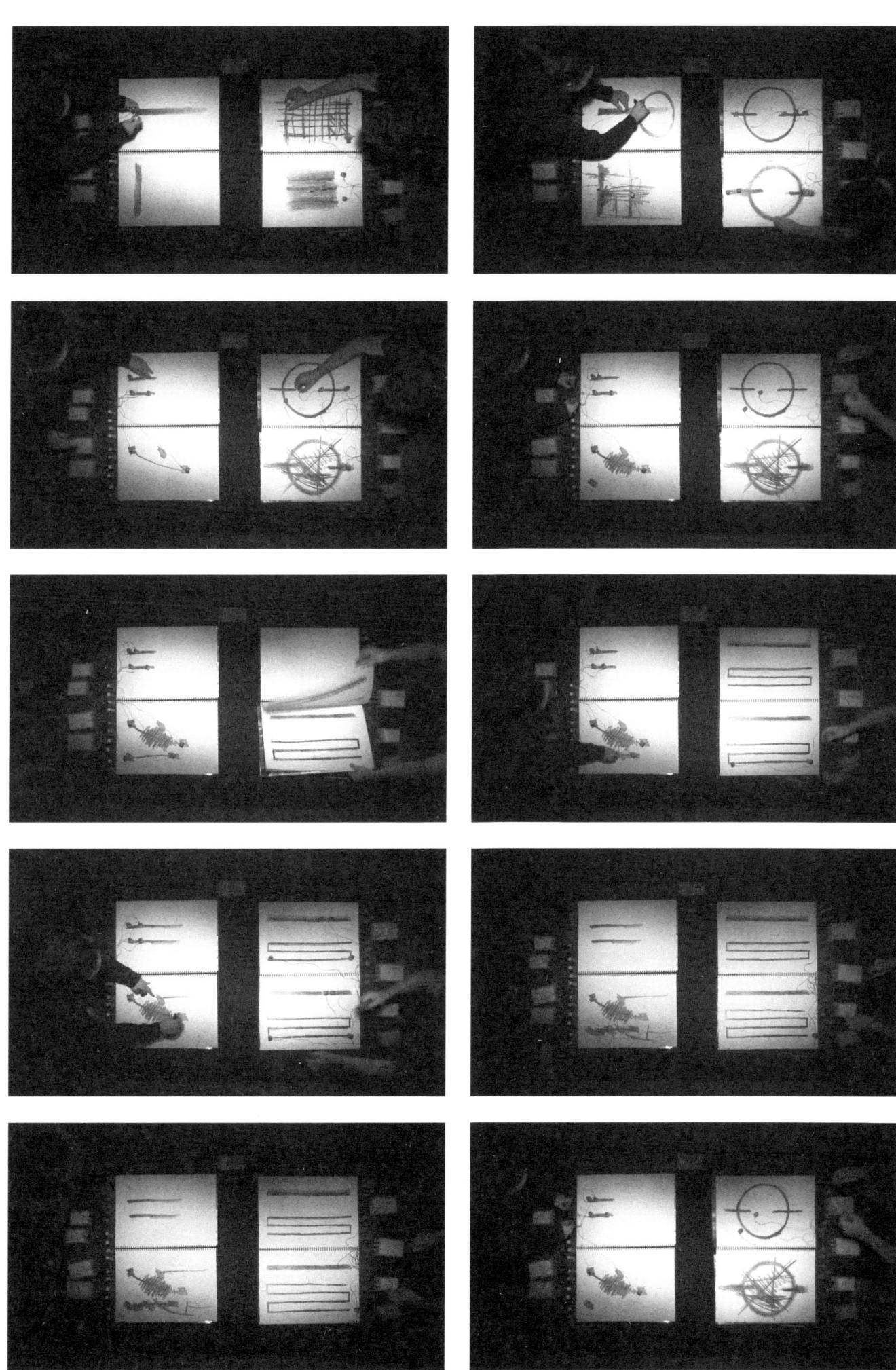

GROUND

"With resistance we grow" is a famous quote of Matthew Barney explaining the outcome of a process in which the artist set limitations to the movement of his body within a space while trying to draw on a piece of paper. These limitations allowed him to understand what the meaning of resistance is and how it leads to creation by the body.

In the same way artists Jeroen Uyttendaele and Dewi de Vree use resistance and their body as a way to create. In their work *Ground* (for which on the occasion this book is made), the artists use graphite, paper, electrodes and amplifiers to create an auditive and visual instrument. By drawing lines or figures on a piece of paper and by adding positive and negative electrodes on the lines, a current flows through the conductive material and a sound is produced. The drawings work much like potentiometers, knobs on an amplifier that regulate volume, pan and pitch.

There are two ways in which the artists work. Either they draw on a large piece of paper or they draw in a book, this way each page forms a different score. The artists sit opposite each other with the paper or book between them, preferably on the floor and in a space where the public can sit around them. Either artist starts with drawing a line or (geometrical) figure on the paper with the graphite, the other follows in an interaction that results in a pattern of lines and figures. Sometimes lines are purposefully erased to create more tension because the length and density (thickness and completeness) of the line translates directly into a variation in the sound. By sliding the electrodes up and down the line, the resistance is changed and the tiny difference in voltage is used to subsequently slide volume, pan and pitch up and down. By adding more lines and electrodes, a multi-layering of frequencies is created, producing the mesmerizing equivalent of a rippling effect you see when you throw many stones in a pool of water. Beauty emerges when (through some action) harmonious chords or overtones are produced, but this is certainly not what the artists are set out to do. The work is all about playing together. But it can also be played alone.

This type of work, creating sound and visual instruments for performance fits the artists's background. Both are products of the famous ArtScience Interfaculty of the University of the Arts, The Hague in the Netherlands (although Dewi also studied at the Gerrit Rietveld Academy in Amsterdam adding to the visual dimensions of the work). This department was once setup by the late Frans Evers together with artist/inventor Dick Raaymakers who envisioned an academy of image and sound. The academy subsequently produced a range of good artists and is notably seen as one of the best academies in the world within its field.

It is for instance Raaymakers who while working for the Dutch company Philips in the late 50's started experimenting with electronics for sound art purposes. With magnetic tape recorders and later synthesizers he searched for the most essential gesture needed for the most minimal sound. Small gestures led to enormous complexity.

But drawing in combination with sound has other art historical connotations too. In the early 70's, Milan Grygar produced his *Acoustic Drawings* in which the process of creating the image was the performance and the creation of a new piece of music. Or the graphic scores of John Cage in which he explored chance and indeterminacy such as in his early composition *Variations I* (1958). This work consisted of six transparent squares, one with 27 dots representing sounds and five with lines representing an assigned musical value. The composition was derived by placing the squares on top of one another in any combination. For Cage anyone could make the music diverting music from skill to chance.

The fact that anyone can make the music is important as well for Uyttendaele and de Vree. Their most recent iteration of *Ground* is the making of a new set of instruments that can be played by anyone, thus adding to chance and indeterminacy of play and composition.

And this is all what the artists are set out to explore, the indeterminacy of play. It makes clear and provokes to investigate that nothing in life is fixed, as the philosopher Catherine Malabou once said that life is determined by its indeterminacy (pointing towards the randomness of natural selection and that we are set out to explore the variability of life by being conscious of it).

You set out to consciously search and understand the improbable world around you and what way of doing that better than to introduce a set of parameters to work with, this could be the graphite, the paper or the addition of players (bodies), but it can also be the space in which the work is performed (sound is produced by air compression). The audience adds another layer to the work. Every aspect adds resistance to the whole and with that both variability and control.

Hicham Khalidi, Brussels, 2015

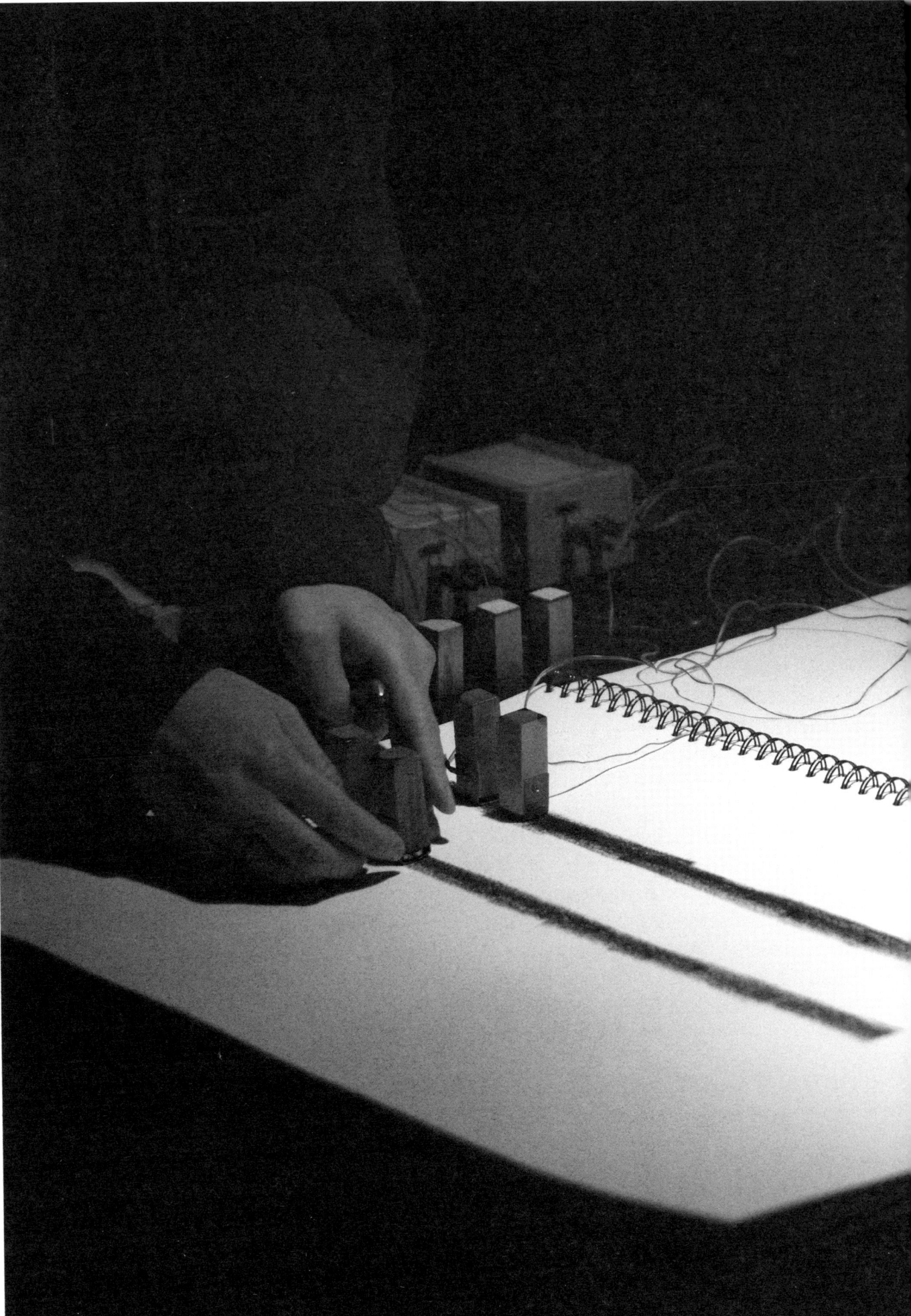

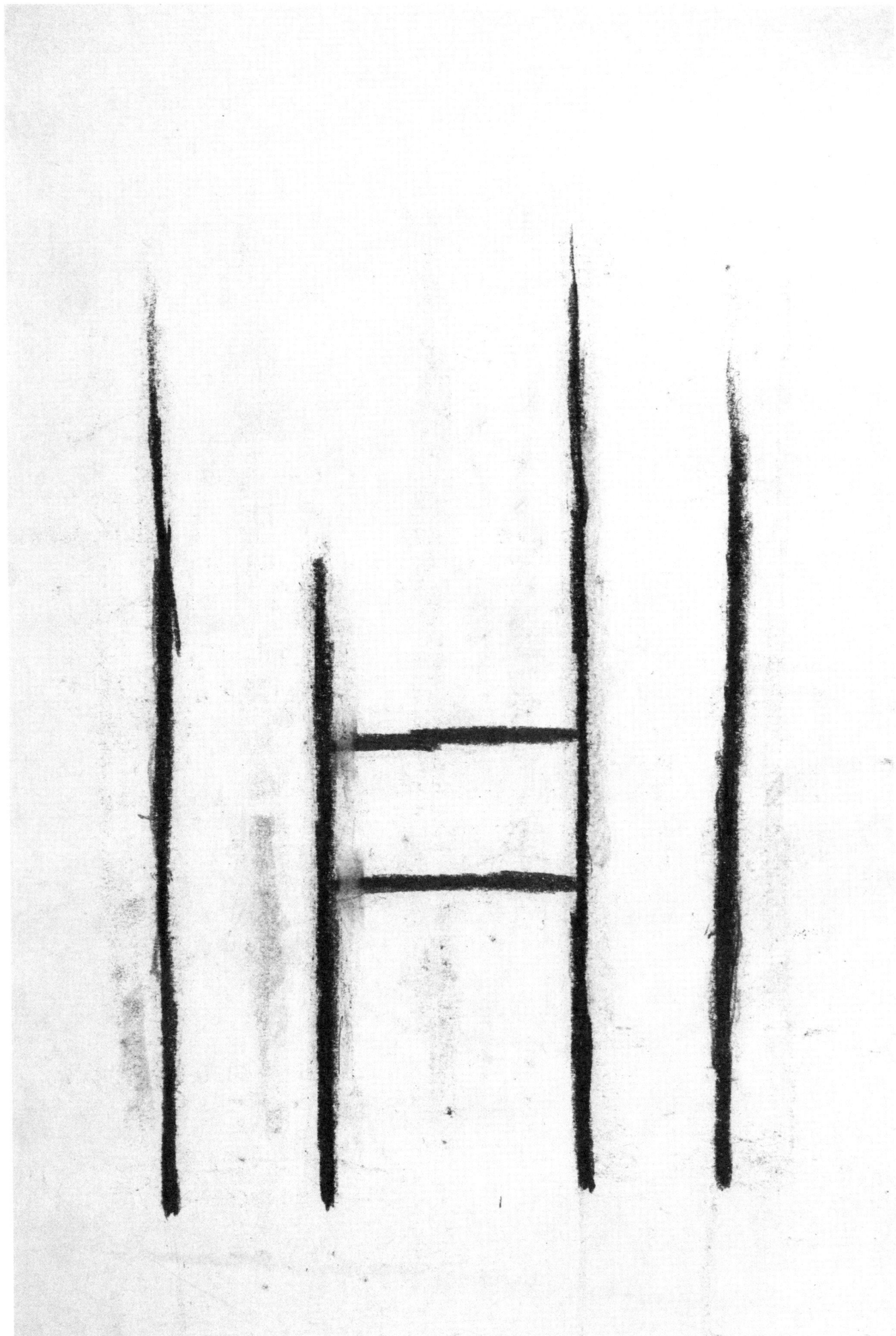

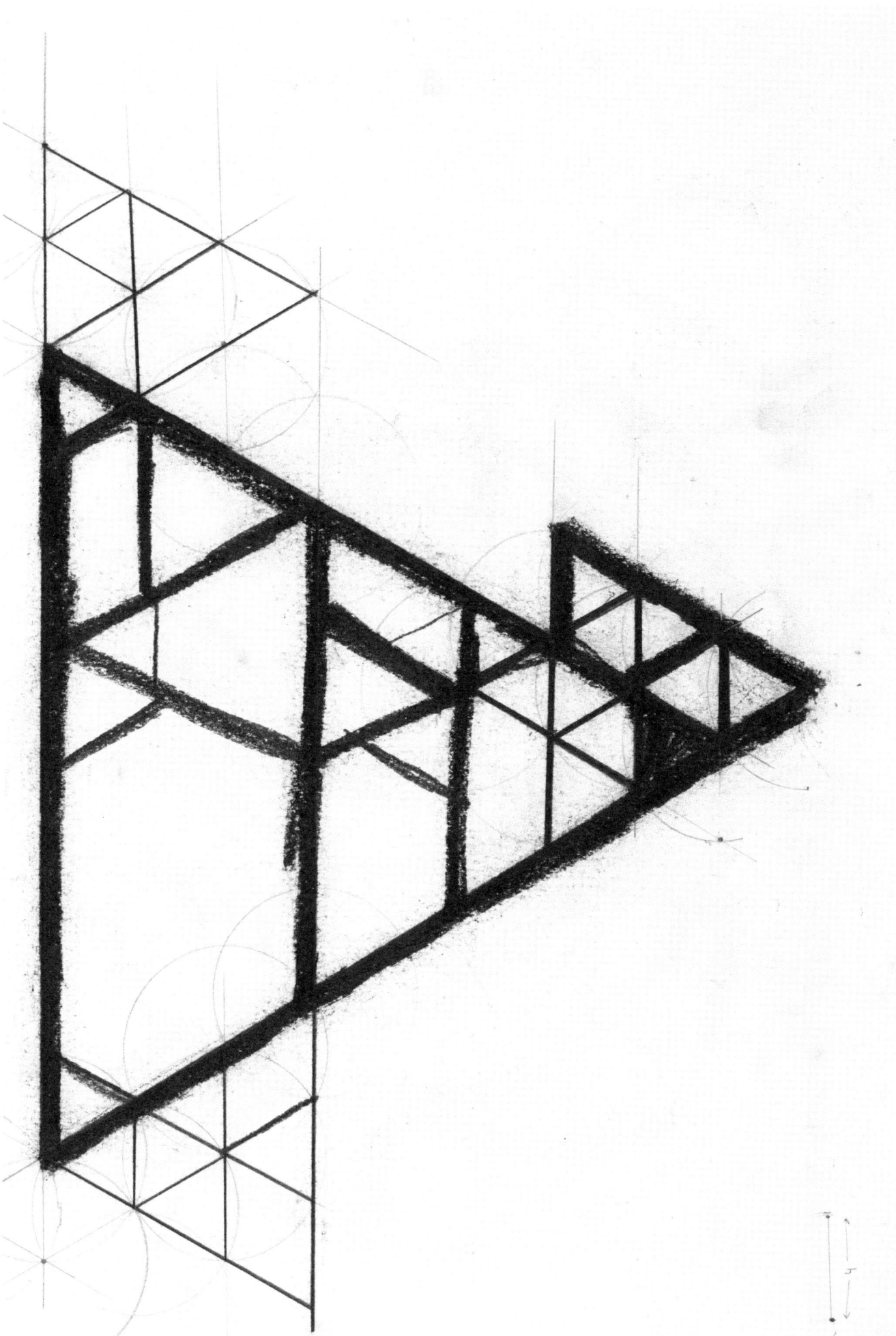

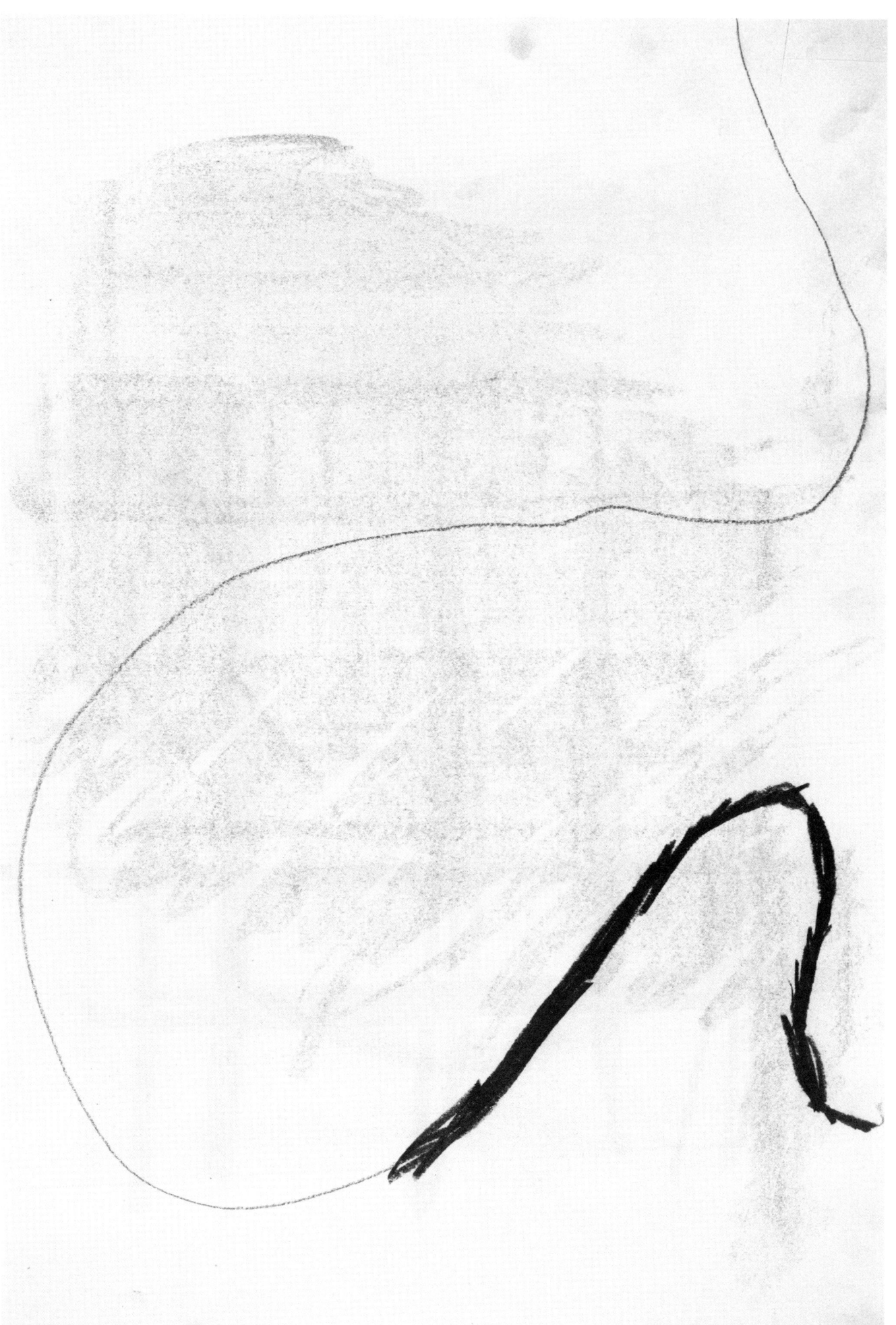